Pioneer
Free Will Baptists
Ministers
Burial Locations
In
Missouri

Copyright 2016
By
Dr. Alton E. Loveless

2020 Update

ISBN 978-1523613175 Soft cover

This book was printed in the United States of America.

To order additional copies of this book, contact:
FWB Publications
Enchanting Acres
1006 Rayme Drive
Columbus, Ohio 43207
Alton.loveless@prodigy.net
Or
www.amazon.com

FWB
FWB Publications

Introduction

Missouri

This book represents all that were part of the Free Will Baptist movement, consisting of the Palmer (south), Randall (north) and others such as the Stone, John-Thomas, John Wheeler Assns., NC OFWB and more.

Many of the photos are poor quality, but it was all I could find. Likewise, I do not have photos or tombstones for many of them. The information about these ministers were all that was available to me or found in archives. I made every effort to include those for which they would be remembered. Some I had no information, but research had shown they were of our denomination.

This Section is taken for a two Volume set done by this author.

Missouri

Rev Ocia Leonard Allen
Birth:
Oct. 6, 1896
Hartville
Wright County
Missouri, USA
Death:
Jun. 1, 1955
Springfield
Greene County
Missouri
Burial:
Greenlawn Memorial Gardens
Springfield
Greene County
Missouri

Ocia Leonard Allen was the son of James "Maudy" Allen, an Iowa Civil War veteran, and Amanda Smith Burton, an Indiana native who moved to Wright County as a child. Both were married before, had families and were widowed.

Ocia served in Europe in WWI, and upon his return in 1920, married Thelma Davis. Their first child was born in Wright County, then by 1923, he moved his family to Fresno, California, where several Burton siblings had already relocated. About 1928, the Allen's returned to Wright County, and eventually moved to Springfield. The Allen family included four sons and a daughter.

In the Mountain Grove, Wright County, Missouri obituary, he was listed as Rev. Allen, having been pastor of churches of Willow Springs and Mansfield, as well as a rural mail carrier.

O. T. Allred
Birth:
Sep. 12, 1895
Death:
Apr. 29, 1976
Burial:
Bethel Cemetery, Masters,
Cedar County, Missouri

Well-known Free Will Baptist preacher and pastor in the Southwest region of the state of Missouri. He was one of the early writers for the Free Will Baptist Gem and was a contemporary with B.F. Brown the first editor. He, with John Rollins, Ken Turner and Winford Davis, were all the early pastors in the Indian Creek Association.

Rev Oliver Truman "Ollie" Allred
BIRTH
12 Sep 1895
Arkansas
DEATH
29 Apr 1976 (aged 80)
Monett, Barry County, Missouri,
BURIAL
Bethel Cemetery
Monett, Barry County, Missouri,

Rev William B. Alsbury
BIRTH
14 Feb 1858
Quincy, Adams County, Illinois
DEATH   19 Apr 1940 (aged 82)
Chillicothe, Livingston County,
Missouri
BURIAL

Edgewood Cemetery
Chillicothe, Livingston County,
Missouri
PLOT   Block 3 Lot 53

Son of John Alsbury. He turned to God in 1883 and received a license to preach in 1886. He was ordained 2 years later. He married Margaret Elizabeth Hartley in 1900. Moved to Chillicothe in 1915 from Pattonsburg, MO. He was a minister for 52 years serving in many churches in north Missouri.

Earl Edward Altis
Birth:
Mar. 14, 1933
Death:
Apr. 12, 1986
Springfield
Greene County, Missouri
Burial:
Providence Cemetery, Cabool,
Texas County, Missouri
He received his bachelor's degree from Southwest Missouri State University in 1961, his Master's degree from the University of Denver in 1964 and an advanced studies certificate in 1974. He was a teacher and librarian in Missouri and Oklahoma colleges and schools. He also served as a Free Will Baptist pastor in Missouri and Colorado. He helped organize the Church Training Services organization in Missouri and served as the editor of the Free Will Baptist Gem. He married Judy Shrewsbury in Nashville, Tennessee in 1979.

Rev Floyd "Bud" Arnold
Birth:
Unknown
Missouri
Death:
Aug. 4, 2016
Springfield
Greene County, Missouri
Burial:
Ozarks Memorial Park
Branson
Taney County, Missouri

Rev. Floyd Arnold, 88 of Branson, died at the Cox South Medical center in Springfield. The services was held at the Friendship FWB church in Branson with Military honors provided by the Vietnam Veterans of American #913 and the United States Army. He ministered many churches in the St. Louis area and Southwest Missouri including the Friendship church where he retired. He also served as Envoy of the Salvation Army in Branson for over 10 years. He is also remembered for his service at Camp Niangua.

Rev James Barker
Birth:
Dec. 17, 1920
Desloge
St. Francois County,
Missouri
Death:
Nov. 6, 2014
Park Hills
St. Francois County
Missouri
Burial:
Hillview Memorial Gardens
Farmington
St. Francois County
Missouri

He was a long time Free Will Baptist minister in the St. Francois QM and one of the most knowledgeable of the history of the oldest conference in Missouri. He pastored many of the churches in this conference and at his death was a member of the Gospel Light Free Will Baptist church. He was married to Geneva, His wife for 73 years. The service was officiated by Rev. Larry Allison and Rev. Herb McMillian.

Lewis P. Barker
Birth:
1913
Death:
Nov. 24, 2002
Oklahoma City,
Okla.
Burial:
Licking Cemetery,
Licking, Texas County, Missouri

He was a member of the First Free Will Baptist Church in Moore, Okla. He pastored FWB churches in Arkansas and Missouri. Surviving are one daughter, Willie Jean Deeds, retired missionary to Brazil, of Moore, Okla.; two sons, Charles Berton Barker of Licking and Dr. Robert Lewis Barker of Oak Park, Calif.

Garland Alexander Barrett
Birth:
Jan. 17, 1854
Ozark County,
Missouri
Death:
May 17, 1900
Ripley County,
Missouri
Burial:
Macedonia Cemetery
Doniphan
Ripley County,
Missouri

He was the co-author with G.W. Million of *A Brief History of the Liberal Baptist People in England and America from 1606 to 1911.*
He was a licentiate at the first meeting of the Social Band thaws

was held with the Sugartee Grove church in Ripley County, Missouri on Sept. 17, 1875. This was the first General Free Will Baptists west of the Mississippi. He was ordained the next year at second association that met with the Brier Crteek church. This Assn. consisted of churches in both Missouri and Arkansas from FWB and General Baptists churches. Barrett was an active member of this conference until his death. He was a noticed writer, preacher, leader and one remembered for his contribution to the denomination. He was the son of John Barrett (1812 - 1883) and Mary Jane Ivy Barrett (1816 - 1870). He married a widow Louisa Jane Flanigan King (1835 - 1894).

Rev David E Bates
Birth:
Mar. 21, 1946
Ironton
Iron County, Missouri
Death:
Dec. 30, 2014
Farmington

St. Francois County, Missouri
Burial:
Hillview Memorial Gardens
Farmington
St. Francois County, Missouri

Reverend David E. Bates of Farmington departed this life and entered into eternity on Tuesday, at his residence at the age of 68 years with his heart prepared to meet his Savior and his guitar in hand. He was born the son of Iva "Aline" (Henson) Bates and the late Paul Elwood Bates. In addition to his father he was preceded in death by a son Jonathan Bates.

David grew up in the Bismarck area and graduated from Bismarck High School in 1964. At the age of eight he met Miss Marilyn Barnes. David and Marilyn quickly became best friends and started a relationship that soon grew into love and the two were married on May 17,1967. He proudly served his country in the Army as an Artillery Sergeant Specialist serving overseas during the Vietnam War. Following his service David returned home, and began a career working as a salesman, and eventually a sales supervisor and trainer for the Bunny Bread Co. then later the Holsum Bakery Co. During this time David attended night school for Business Management, and later enrolled in Bible College by correspondence at Hillsdale College. In 1977 he received the call to the Gospel Ministry and was ordained in the Free Will Baptist Church. He served at the Free Will Baptist Church in Farmington as an associate pastor and music director and in Santa Paula, CA. as senior pastor. In 2008, he became the pastor of Grace Community Church in Knob Lick where he served until the time of his death.

David was an amazingly talented musician and enjoyed singing and playing music for church, his family, and friends. While serving as Music Director at Farmington First Free Will Baptist Church, he was also the director and a member of the Gospel Quartet "Master Peace" performing at various local churches and community events. A memorial service at Grace Community Church at the Nelson Music City Theater at Knob Lick. Interment with full military honors was at Hillview Memorial Gardens in Farmington.

Harry Howard Beatty
Birth:
Aug. 16, 1911
Oregon County, Missouri
Death:
Feb. 27, 1994
Owasso,
Tulsa County, Oklahoma
Burial:
Thayer Cemetery, Thayer,
Oregon County, Missouri

Beatty was converted at the age 19 and began his ministry in the Thayer area. He was a well-known Freewill Baptist minister for many years in Missouri and Oklahoma as a pastor and church planter. He was the first Missouri Promotional Secretary of Free Will Baptist and served in that capacity from 1961 until 1975. During his tenure led the state of Missouri in becoming one of the strongest co-operative giving states in the denomination.

Lue Bequette
Birth:
Apr. 16, 1922
Death:
Jan. 4, 2008
Burial:
Mine La Motte Cemetery,
Mine La Motte,
Madison County,
Missouri
He was an early Free Will Baptist minister and pastored in the St. Francois Association in Southeast Missouri.

Manuel Eugene Bingham
Birth:
May 7, 1924
Death:
Apr. 22, 2007
Burial:
New Home Cemetery, Falcon,
Laclede County, Missouri
He worked as a cattle farmer and in the timber. Manuel followed the Free Will Baptist faith throughout the years.

Mansfield Edward Bingham
BIRTH
8 Jun 1833
Johnson County, Arkansas, USA
DEATH
5 Feb 1913 (aged 79)
Laclede County, Missouri, USA
BURIAL
Bingham Cemetery
Laclede County, Missouri, USA

Mansfield Edward "Ed" Bingham was the son of Harman Bingham and Sally Mitchell. He married Martha E. Weir about 1862 and Milla "Millie" E. Myers March 18, 1897 in Laclede Co., Missouri. He was a private in Company H Missouri Cavalry of the Union Army. He was the father of six children. He was an ordained minister. Military Record and a Book confirm the following: Mansfield E. Bingham, age 30, a farmer, born in Johnson County,

Arkansas, enlisted with the 8th Missouri Volunteer Cavalry, USA on March 9, 1864 in Springfield, Missouri as a Recruit for DeVall's Bluff, Arkansas in Company "H". August 27, 1864 Absent, On Scout Duty. October 30, 1864 Absent, On Scout Duty. July 22, 1865 Transferred to Company "H", of the 11th Missouri Volunteer Cavalry, USA per War Department Special Order # 172 to complete a -3- Year enlistment.

Otho A. Boyd
BIRTH
18 Jun 1920
DEATH
8 Oct 2006 (aged 86)
BURIAL
Ozark Memorial Park Cemetery
Joplin, Jasper County, Missouri

Pastored in the Indian Creek Assn. Also pastored in Oklahoma.

Miles Evans Brasher
Birth:
Sep. 6, 1855
Death:
Feb. 23, 1948
Burial:
Crossroads Cemetery,
Lebanon,
Laclede County,
Missouri

Nathan Joseph Breshears
Birth:
Jun. 15, 1863
Missouri
Death:

Dec. 11, 1936
Springfield
Greene County, Missouri
Burial:
Greenlawn Memorial Gardens
Springfield
Greene County,
Missouri

K. Breshears and Mary Ann McDonald. According to his death certificate, he died of apoplexy and hypertension. His occupation was minister.

Benjamin F. Brown

Birth:
Jan. 6, 1870
Death:
Aug. 29, 1964
Barry County, Missouri
Burial:
Purdy Cemetery, Purdy,
Barry County, Missouri

Rev. B. F. Brown was the second president of Tecumseh College in Tecumseh, Oklahoma until after 1927 when the school burned. At that time there was a committee considering a publication that would be located in Missouri, but a publication for everyone in the denomination. This committee offered B. F. Brown the opportunity to be the first editor, even though he still resided in Tecumseh. The first issues of the *Free Will Baptist GEM* were published in Tecumseh, beginning January 1929. In May of 1930 the paper was moved to Purdy, Missouri. Rev. Brown moved to Purdy and continued as editor until 1939 when he retired. At that time, the publication was moved to Monett, Missouri. However, in 1946 he was called upon to rescue the magazine and became the acting editor from December of 1946 until August of 1947.B. F. Brown during the time between 1929 until 1935 had become a leader in the Cooperative Association which existed throughout the Midwest. It later was to merge with the General Conference, a conference mainly in the Southeast, in 1935 at Nashville, Tennessee. Rev. Brown would sign for the Cooperative Association to accept the agreement with the General Conf. This agreement in 1935 formed the National Association of Free Will Baptists. Rev. Brown was a member of the executive board and served as its secretary. Later, he became a member of the Home Missions Board of the National Convention. Records revealed that he attended the national convention until about 1946.

Claude R Bryan

Birth:
May 13, 1884
Death:
Nov. 26, 1981
Burial:
Thayer Cemetery, Thayer,
Oregon County, Missouri

He was an early Free Will Baptist preacher in the south-central part of the state of Missouri.

He received license to preach in 1874, and was ordained in 1875. His work was in Michigan, Iowa, and Missouri. He assisted in organizing four churches. He pastored the Clay and Delhi churches.

Rev. George BULLOCK, was the son of William and Nancy (Heten) BULLOCK. He was married July 28, 1861, to Sarah Aldrich, daughter of Jefferson and Eliza ALDRICH.

Rev George Bullock
Birth:
Jan. 31, 1837
Ontario, Canada
Death:
Jul. 19, 1932
Pierce City
Lawrence County
Missouri
Burial:
Pierce City Cemetery
Pierce City
Lawrence County
Missouri

James Eli Burney
Birth:
Dec. 20, 1879
Wright County
Missouri
Death:
Mar. 10, 1951
Mountain Grove
Wright County
Missouri
Burial:
Steele Memorial Cemetery
Hartville
Wright County
Missouri

James "Eli" Burney was the son of William Lafayette Burney and Sarah Ann [Cope] Burney.

He married Ora Alice Claxton, daughter of James Edward Claxton and Phoebe Carolina [Palmer] Claxton, 14/Jan/1900 in Wright County, Missouri.

Birth:
November 23, 1926
Paragould, Arkansas
Death:
November 7, 2019
Washington Care Center,
Greenville, Mississippi.
Burial:
Myrtle Cemetery
Myrtle, Missouri

He was born, to Clarence Hall Burton and Maude Smith Burton. On March 4, 1950, he was married at Myrtle, Missouri, to Wilma Vivian Wisehart, who preceded him in death on August 21, 2011. He and Vivian were blessed with two sons, Steve and John. Mr. Burton graduated from Oak Grove High School, Paragould, Arkansas in 1944. Reverend Burton served on various state boards in the Arkansas and Missouri State Associations. He served as moderator of the Missouri State Association from 1970-1973. He served on the National Board of Sunday School and Church Training for four years and served twelve years on the Trustee Board, Free Will Baptist Bible College. Reverend Burton served as pastor of the Ballew's Chapel Church Grubbs, Arkansas from 1955 – 1960; he accepted the pastorate of the First Church in Fredericktown, Missouri in 1960 and was there until October 1963, when he began his work as pastor of the First Church in Berkeley, Missouri. He served the Berkeley Church twelve years and in July, 1975 accepted the position of Executive Secretary for the Missouri State Association and filled this position for seventeen years, resigning this work in July 1992 and semi-retired. He also served as Assistant pastor at United Freewill Baptist Church, West Plains from May 1997 until September 2011. Clarence served his country faithfully in the military. First, he served with the 11th Airborne, as a part of the Occupational Forces in Japan. At the completion of that tour of duty he was honorably discharged. Later, he joined the Air Force Reserve and during the Korean War was recalled to active duty to serve with the 3310th Technical Training Wing of the 5th Air Force. At the end of this tour of duty he was honorably discharged.

He is survived by two sons, Steve Burton and wife, Vickie, Greenville, Mississippi and John Burton and wife, Dianne, Imperial, Missouri.

Cecil Herbert Campbell
Birth:
Sep. 28, 1910
Stella,
Newton County,
Missouri
Death:
Jul. 18, 1999
North Little Rock,
Pulaski County, Arkansas
Burial:
Jones Chapel Cemetery,
Stella,
Newton County, Missouri

He served churches in Missouri and North Carolina. He conducted revivals in Texas, Oklahoma, Missouri, North and South Carolina. He was an active denominational leader on state and national levels, with a good ministry wherever he served.

John M Carnahan, Sr
Birth:
Jun. 7, 1877
Death:
May 3, 1954
Burial:
Maple Park Cemetery
Springfield
Greene County, Missouri

Early FWB Preacher.

Rev Jacob Newton Carner
Birth:
Dec. 8, 1838
Indiana
Death:
Apr. 13, 1919
Howell County, Missouri
Burial:
Merideth/Meredith Cemetery
Lanton
Howell County, Missouri

He was a preacher of the General Baptists of Kentucky when he as accepted as a minister in the Social Band Assn. in Arkansas where he was a leader. He did a great work as he remained but afterwards moved to Howell County, Missouri and rejoined the General Baptists. He was a veteran of Co H 8 Ky Cav Union Army. He was married twice to Francis Prudence Tackett Carner (1841 - 1925) and Nancy E Jones Carner (1841 - 1904).

Elijah Carpenter
Birth:
1858
Illinois
Death:
1941
Seymour
Webster County, Missouri
Burial:
Liberty Cemetery Seymour
Webster County, Missouri

Rev Eli Miller Chandler, Sr
BIRTH
16 Feb 1850
Ste. Genevieve County, Missouri, USA
DEATH
1910 (aged 59–60)
Missouri, USA
BURIAL
Little Vine Church Cemetery
Ste. Genevieve County, Missouri,

CHANDLER, Rev. E.M., son of Jonathan and Elizabeth (Harris) Chandler. He was converted in 1868, and ordained in 1886. His work has been that of an evangelist. He was married March

14, 1877 to Nancy A. Lunsford,"---taken from "Free Baptist Cyclopedia," pub. 1889, by Burgess and Ward, pg. 109

Mike S. Cleaver
Birth:
Nov. 21, 1897
Death:
Dec. 6, 1971
Burial:
Oakside Cemetery,
Summersville,
Shannon County, Missouri

Rev Marion Benjamin Clift
Birth:
Mar. 17, 1873
Webster County,Missouri
Death:
Dec. 1, 1926
Webster County, Missouri
Burial:
Black Oak Cemetery
Marshfield
Webster County, Missouri

Early Free Will Bapt. minister ordained in Sept. 1909.

Fred E Comber
Birth:
1857
Canada
Death:
1917
Galveston
Galveston County. Texas
Burial:
Weiss Cemetery
Doe Run
St. Francois County, Missouri

Born in Canada; immigrated to Bonne Terre, Mo. to work as an engineer at about 18 years of age. Married Elizabeth Weiss of Doe Run about 1885. About 1895 he began preaching and helped to organize Free Baptist Churches. He had served the Free Baptist Churches at Doe Run, MO, Murphysboro and Ava, IL and various other localities in this area as well as southern Illinois. He was preceded in death by his wife Elizabeth early in 1915, after which he located in the Galveston, TX area for health reasons and where he had accepted a pastorate.

Funeral Services were conducted by his friend and co-worker of many years, Reverend George Gordon of Ava, IL.

Note: per Gib Weiss - a neighbor's team of Percheron horses were used to skid the tombstone up to the cemetery.

Tombstone was donated by some of his parishioner's (from another state) and shipped to the Weiss farm in Doe Run..

Rev. Fred E. Comber was in a list of ministers who had pastored the First FWB Church in Bryan, TX; he from 1915-1917.

Elizabeth Weiss Comber
BIRTH
14 Dec 1855
St. Francois County, Missouri, USA
DEATH
7 Mar 1915 (aged 59)
BURIAL
Weiss Cemetery
Doe Run, St. Francois County,
Missouri, USA

3rd child of Heinrich & Mary Elizabeth Weiss. Married Fred Comber of Canada about 1885. She was also a free will Baptist lady minister and according to Illinois records Elizabeth Comber pastored the Lauder & Dry Hill churches and supplied at the Percy church

Archie Stanley Cooper
Birth:
Jul. 10, 1907
Mystic
Sullivan County, Missouri
Death:
Apr. 27, 2003
Kirksville
Adair County, Missouri
Burial:
Green Grove Cemetery
Novinger
Adair County, Missouri

Reverend Archie Cooper, 95, passed away at Kirksville Manor Care Center in Kirksville.

The son of Byron Isaac and Cleo Virginia (Muncy) Cooper. On October 16, 1927, Archie was united in marriage to Verdie Summers and to this union two daughters were born. Verdie preceded Archie in death in 1945. In 1946 he was united in marriage to Gladys Wellman Peterson who preceded Archie in death on January 30, 1997.

Reverend Cooper lived most of his life in Adair County and was a preacher of fifty-three years. Archie was ordained for the ministry by the Free Will Baptist Association at Hazel Creek Church in Adair County on September 4, 1937. He served at the New Harmony Baptist Church from 1938 to 1947 and at age eighty-two, returned to Pastor from 1966 until the early 90's. He also ministered at Low Ground, Baring, Refuge, Jewel and Sublette church's. Archie also spent thirty-two years every morning, six days a week at 6:15 a.m. serving many counties on KIRX with his morning meditations that he thought of from scripture, prayer and often a poem. Throughout Archie's amazing career, he ministered over 900 weddings and 2800 funerals.

Archie was recently recognized as the KTVO Heartland Hero.

Reverend Archie was a devoted member of the New Harmony Baptist Church.

Funeral services was held at in Kirksville with the Rev. Daniel Eloe officiating.

Rev W. H. Copas
Birth:
Sep. 9, 1836
Ohio
Death:
Jul. 23, 1904
Missouri
Burial:
Niangua Cemetery
Niangua
Webster County, Missouri

The St. Francois County, Fed U.S. Census in 1880 Fth VA Mth Pa Wife Mary A 40 OH, Son William He stated his Occupation as Shoe Maker which most ministers had a trade in which to a living. In 1890 Mo. Vets. Census, it showed W.H. Copass, a native of Ohio was working in Missouri with Rev O.S. Harding of Iowa and Dr. E.H. Hunt in beginning new churches in Missouri. His SON Charles K. Copas IS BURIED IN THIS Cemetery.

And with unfaltering lip and heart, I call the Saviour mine.

Henry Clay Crase
Birth:
1865
Death:
1966
Burial:
Garfield Cemetery,
Garfield,
Oregon County, Missouri
He had a long ministry in the Free Will Baptist denomination and was very active as a district and state leader.

Grover Cleveland Cravens
Birth:
Feb. 3, 1885
Wright County
Missouri
Death:
Nov. 22, 1958
Mansfield
Wright County
Missouri
Burial:
Steele Memorial Cemetery
Hartville
Wright County Missouri

William Elvin Crews
Birth:
Sep. 22, 1893 Alton, Oregon
County,
Missouri
Death:
Aug. 24, 1946 Oregon County,
Missouri
Burial:
Shiloh Cemetery, Alton,
Oregon County, Missouri

He was a Veteran of the U.S Army (Pvt; Btry D, 342 Inf) serving in World War I. Minister of the Freewill Baptist Church.

Rev John H Culley
Birth:
Jan. 29, 1839
Jackson County
Illinois
Death:
Apr. 23, 1907
St. Francois County
Missouri
Burial:
Doe Run Memorial Cemetery
Doe Run
St. Francois County, Missouri
Plot: Sect. C

Rev. John H. Culley, was an ordained minister of the Freewill Baptist Church. He married Clarinda Rhodes. Oct. 9, 1861,
and served in various offices of trust in the town of Murphysborough, Ill., until his conversion in 1876. He then devoted himself to ministerial work, receiving ordination Dec. 27, 1878. He has ministered to the Beaver Pond, Mt. Nebo.
Drura, De Soto, Rock Springs and Cedar churches, all in the Looney Springs Q. M., Ill., the three first named having been organized by himself; and in the St. Francois Q. M., Missouri.
He was in the sixth session of the Missouri State Conference of FWB, which minutes are dated Oct. 8, 1896, when convened at the Casteel Church in Clinton Co. MO, and his name is listed as being from Doe Run. During the 1890 session of the State Conference Rev. John H. Culley, was re-elected as president. This old conference was affiliated with northern Randall movement.

There is a Civil War record of John H. Culley, as Commissary Sgt, Pvt. Illinois 18th Inf., Co. CFS.

Rev Jack C. Day

Birth: May 26, 1934
Niangua
Webster County
Missouri
Death: Feb. 9, 2016
Springfield
Greene County
Missouri
Burial:
Marshfield Cemetery
Marshfield
Webster County
Missouri

He was born to Orville and Mabel Whitehead Day. Jack was the eighth child born unto a family of nine children.

On May 21, 1955, he married Freda Mae Sell, and to this union was born one daughter, Carolyn. Jack and Freda were married for 60 years.

Jack was a loyal servant for Jesus Christ. He learned as a young adult that he had been called to spread the Gospel of our Lord. In addition to a career at Custom Trailer/Polar, He pastored Black Oak Freewill Baptist Church in Marshfield for over 48 years. While he tirelessly served the members of Black Oak, he also was a spiritual comfort to many others in the community.

Rev Henry B Davis

Birth:
Jun. 30, 1819
Warren County
New York
Death:
Jul. 4, 1879
Warren County
New York
Burial:
Highland Cemetery
Hamilton
Caldwell County
Missouri

He commenced preaching in 1847. His labors were mostly in the Caldwell and other churches of Lake George Quarterly Meeting except two years at Ashfield, Mass, where he was ordained [Freewill Baptist], Sept. 13, 1857, by a council of the Renesselear, Q.M. He was well received as a minister and quite successful.

Elizabeth Crawshaw on 4 Feb 1872 in Briar Creek, Ripley Co, MO.

And their children were Grace Davis Burlison (1838 - 1890), Samuel W Davis (1839 - 1885), Eliphaz Davis (1845 - 1925), Van Crawshaw Davis (1847 - 1928), Daniel L. Davis (1849 - 1917), and Joshua Dial Crawshaw Davis (1854 - 1934).

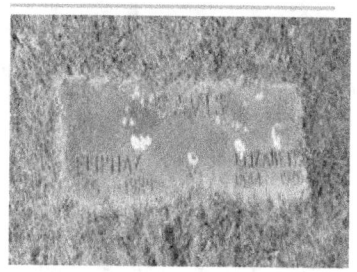

Eliphaz Davis
Birth:
Aug. 23, 1845
Jackson County, Illinois
Death:
Aug. 9, 1925
Everett
Snohomish County
Washington
Burial:
Ledbetter Cemetery
Pottersville
Howell County, Missouri

An early FWB Minister serving in the General Free Will Baptist Assn. His parents were Van B. and Eliza Crawford Crawshaw Davis. He wed

Samuel W Davis
Birth:
Aug. 13, 1839
Death:
Mar. 4, 1885
Burial:
Shirley Cemetery
Briar
Ripley County, Missouri

An Early FWB minister serving in the General Free Will Baptist Assn. which was an association of General Baptists and Free Will Baptists in Missouri and Arkansas.He was a brother to Eliphaz Davis who was also a preacher in this movement.

Winford C. Davis
Birth:
Dec. 8, 1904
Death:
May 5, 1997
Burial:
Bethel Cemetery, Monett,
Barry County, Missouri

Davis lived to be 93 years old and had been a Free Will Baptist preacher for more than 70 years in which time he was a very active leader in the denomination.

He was converted at age 12 at a brush arbor revival. He preached his first sermon in the Macedonia Free Will Baptist Church in 1926 and was a member of that church at the time of his death. He pastored churches for 60 years including 40 years at the Macedonia church in various tenures. He served for 19 years as Secretary-Treasurer of the Missouri State Association. He was a member of the National Board Of Education that led the denomination to establish the Free Will Baptist Bible College. He was Secretary-Treasurer of the Foreign Missions Board and made three trips to Cuba: in 1942; in 1944; and in 1946. He helped to establish Missouri's magazine, *THE GEM*, and served 3 1/2 years as its editor and manager from a printing office in Monett. He kept a comprehensive record of his ministry which recorded he had preached 9,100 sermons, won 2,170 souls to the Lord, and received 1,385 members into the church. He traveled 330,772 miles, not counting three trips to Cuba and three trips to Israel. He conducted 159 revivals, officiated at 173 weddings, and conducted 621 funerals. He organized 13 churches, baptized 40, and ordained 30 deacons. He attended the organizational meeting of the National Association in 1935 and was a member of the Treaties Committee. He was truly a pioneer within the Free Will Baptist denomination.

Christian Benjamin Dees
Birth:
Jun. 28, 1902 Fredericktown,
Madison County, Missouri
Death:
May 19, 1973
St. Louis City, Missouri
Burial:
Woodlawn Cemetery,
Leadington,
St. Francois County,
Missouri

An active pastor and leader in Missouri. He was editor of the Free Will Baptist Gem, serving in that position for a number of years. He was a member of the St. Francios Association in South East Missouri.

Alice M Dickey
Birth:
1907
Death:
2001
Burial:
White Chapel Memorial Gardens,
Springfield,
Greene County, Missouri

She was a longtime minister and known for founding the First Free Will Baptist Church of Kansas City, Missouri.

Claude A. Dotson
Birth:
Aug. 23, 1891
Death:
Apr. 29, 1954
Burial:
Huddleston Cemetery,

Alton,
Oregon County, Missouri

An early Free Will Baptist pastor in south central Missouri.

Rev. Sammy Dismang
Birth:
March 30, 1942
Lebanon, Missouri
Death:
October 21, 2019
Mercy Hospital, Lebanon, Missouri
Burial:
Unknown

Sammy was a son of Chester and Vena Richardson Dismang. He was married Patsy L. Perry March 23, 1961 and they had one son. He lived his entire life in Laclede County and was a truck driver for the Frisco company, then owned and operated the Downtown Furniture Store, since 1977, he has been an auctioneer. He was a long-time pastor of several area churches and was the pastor of the

Unity Worship Center at his passing.

William Duponit Dowell
Birth:
Oct. 5, 1880
Philadelphia
Philadelphia County, Pennsylvania
Death:
Feb. 25, 1950
Camden County
Missouri
Burial:
Hopewell Cemetery
Tunas
Dallas County,
Missouri

Early FWB preacher in the General Free Will Baptist Assn.

William Driver, Sr
Birth:
1859
Jefferson City, Missouri
Death:
1934
Burial:
Iberia Cemetery, Iberia
Miller County, Missouri

Was born in in 1859, the son of a slave woman named Amanda/Mandy Dixon. At an early age he was adopted by a black family named Driver and carried that name the rest of his life. William Driver, Sr. moved to Laclede Co., MO in the early 1880's and located near the small town of Eldridge. He became a preacher in the Free Will Baptist Church and traveled around central Missouri as an evangelist. About 1916 he moved his wife and children to Miller County and located southwest of Iberia near the Pleasant Hill community and the old Rankin Wright Cemetery. Driver was a well-known minister in the area as he traveled around preaching the Holy Word and playing loudly on his large drum. When he died in 1934, his funeral was held at the Iberia Nazarene Church, conducted by Rev. Otto Shearrer. He was buried at the Iberia Cemetery (per his obituary) but no stone marks his grave today.

Eunice S. *Jenkerson* Edwards
Birth:
Jan. 5, 1912
Death:
Jul. 30, 1997
St. Francois County, Missouri
Burial:
Parkview Cemetery, Farmington,
St. Francois County, Missouri

She served as pastor at the Leadington Freewill Baptist Church in Missouri and then she served the National Free Will Baptist Women's Auxiliary for seven years as Director. A great leader and servant of God.

Rev William B. Fadely
Birth:
Dec. 8, 1865
Death:
Aug. 1, 1946
Burial:
Hopewell Cemetery
DeKalb County
Missouri

Rev. William B. Fadely, was an ordained Free Will Baptist minister. He attended the 1924 session of the Cooperative General Association of FWB, in Tecumseh, OK, and listed his home as 'Weatherby, MO'. [DeKalb Co].

Thomas Campbell Ferguson
Birth: Jan. 10, 1870
Ontario, Canada
Death: Mar. 28, 1957
Gallatin
Daviess County
Missouri
Burial:
Alta Vista Cemetery
Alta Vista
Daviess County
Missouri

Thomas Campbell Ferguson was the son of William Ferguson, and Jessie (McFarland) Ferguson. He departed this life at the Sullivan Rest Home in Gallatin, MO, March 28, 1957, at the age of 87 years, 2mos, and 17 days.

His early life was spent between farmhand, sailor, miner and railroading.

At the age of 26 years he was converted and took an active part in Christian work, from that time he attended the Moody Bible school in Chicago. From there he went to Wisconsin, and while there he united with the Freewill Baptist Church in which he was ordained a minister in the year, 1900, at Lincoln, Neb., and spent the most of his life in evangelical and pastoral work. He baptized more than 2000 people and aided in many ordinations.

He was a friend and associate of Rev. John H. Wolfe, Neb., and he joined with Wolfe in leading in the formation of the Cooperative General Association, and before that, the Southwestern Free Will Baptist Convention (of Texas, Oklahoma, and Missouri). Rev. Ferguson, as a delegate from Texas at the time, joined with Wolfe in opposing the merger of the Randall movement Freewill Baptists with the Northern Baptists in 1910. Rev. Ferguson was on the original Board of Trustees of Tecumseh College, Oklahoma, when it was founded by the Cooperative General Association in 1917, and Rev. John H. Wolfe was elected president.

Rev. Ferguson also helped to organize the Missouri State Association of Free Will Baptists, and was elected moderator of it for several years, as well as serving as State Evangelist of Missouri FWB for some time.

He held revival meetings in several states and in parts of Canada. The most of his work was done in Missouri, Kansas, Texas and Nebraska.

He was united in marriage to Miss Myrtle Henderson in 1900. To this union three children were born. He was later united in marriage April 25, 1932, to Miss Odessa Reid. Funeral services were conducted by Eld. John D. McKown, of Daviess Co., March 30, at the Alta Vista church after which he was laid to rest in the cemetery nearby. [Alta Vista Cemetery].

Charley David Findley
Birth:
Jul. 25, 1891
Death:
Sep. 17, 1972
Burial:
Pleasant Hill Cemetery
Hartville
Wright County

Rev William Henry Ford, Sr
Birth:
Nov. 18, 1838
Warren County
Tennessee
Death:
Jun. 27, 1905
Pea Ridge
Benton County, Arkansas
Burial:
Jane Cemetery
McDonald County, Missouri

Brothers who were FWB ministers in Arkansas and Texas. George Harvey Ford (1827 - 1896). Richard E. Ford (1835 - 1922). William Henry Ford (1838 - 1905). James Alexander Ford (1842 - 1912). Josephus Wesley Ford (1848 - 1898). Markley Stanford Ford (1852 - 1917).

Warren Franklin
Birth:
Mar. 12, 1879
Osseo, Wisconsin
Death:
May 25, 1957
Burial:
Lone Rock Cemetery,
Plad,
Dallas County, Missouri

He was an early Free Will Baptist minister.

Jerry William Fields
Birth:
May 19, 1934
Springfield
Greene County, Missouri
Death:
Oct. 1, 2014
Greene County, Missouri
Burial:
Robberson Prairie Cemetery
Ebenezer
Greene County, Missouri

Jerry William Fields, departed this life surrounded by loved at Mercy Hospital in Springfield, Mo. He was 80 years and 4 months old.

Jerry was born to Ernest E. and Bernice (Tidwell) Fields at their home in Springfield. Jerry married Dorlene Deeds on May 10, 1951 in Harrison, Ark. and to this union four children were born.

While at a rodeo Jerry met Dorlene, the love of his life, beside an old watering pump. Years later the eyes of his understanding were opened in a little hotel room as he read a Gideon Bible. Jerry's love of God, family and his commitment to every good work laid a foundation for his children and succeeding generations. Jerry was described by his family as a servant, teacher, a man of great love, a pastor and father devoted to the truth and speaking the truth in love. In his words, "I am too blessed to be depressed".

He created a lifetime of memories that will be treasured in the hearts and minds of his family and those he pastored for over fifty years.

Howard Eugene Filkins,
Botn:
Feb. 18,1933
Sublette, Mo.
Death:
Aug. 31, 2019
OKC, OK
Burial:
Hazel Creek Union Cemetery NW
Kirksville, MO

He was born to Boyd H. and Lola P. (Peterson) Filkins (deceased). He married Barbara Joan (Jody) Barnett on December 25, 1955. He served in U.S. Army Ordinance from 1954-1957 active duty and 1957-1962 in the reserves.

Memorial services at CrossPointe Church, in Norman, OK.

Memorials chosen are Free Will Baptist International Missions or 1040i (humanitarian organization). Memorial donations may be left at or mailed to Travis-Noe Funeral Home, P.O. Box 306, Kirksville, MO 63501

Rev Perry Thomas Gardenhire
Birth:
Feb. 10, 1908
Death:
Oct. 6, 1997
Burial:
Idumea Cemetery
Laquey
Pulaski County
Missouri

A Free Will Baptist minister who pastored churches in Calif. before he retired. His name appears from Exeter, CA, in the 1967 Southern Association No. 1. Remembered here.

Rev Thomas A Gaines
Birth:
May 15, 1846
Washington
Wilkes County,
Georgia
Death: 1907
Missouri
Burial:
Hickory Creek
Jameson
Daviess County,Missouri

Levi Jackson Gearing
Birth:
Apr. 17, 1881
Missouri
Death:
Oct. 30, 1945

Burial:
Coldwater Cemetery
Manes
Wright County
Missouri

Spouse: Sophia Elizabeth Long Gearing (1882 - 1939)

Rev Ken Goff
Birth:
Oct. 16, 1939
Savonburg
Allen County, Kansas
Death: Nov. 15, 2014
Bonne Terre
St. Francois County, Missouri
Burial:
Three Rivers Baptist Church
Cemetery
Farmington
St. Francois County, Missouri

Mildred Gilliam
Birth
Death
Burial
Greentop Memorial Park
Greentop,
Schuyler Co.,
Missouri

Pastor of New Harmon
FWB Church, Kirksville, Mo.

He retired in 2011 from being and active minister for 41 years, and also being the superintendent at the Free Will Baptist Youth Camp in Niangua, Missouri, for 16 years. He was a member of the Parkview Free Will Baptist Church in Desloge, Missouri. The Rev.'s Gary Parker, Lindell Richardson and Ron DeGonia Officiated.

Ross H. Green
Birth:
May 7, 1929
Death:
Apr. 28, 1989
Burial:
Parrack Grove Cemetery,
Macks Creek,
Camden County, Missouri
He was a veteran and Cpl in the US Air Force. He was a minister & pastor in the Free Will Baptist denomination.

Francis Marion Goodnight
BIRTH
14 Aug 1847
Greene County, Missouri
DEATH
19 Jan 1890
BURIAL
Goodnight Cemetery
Purdy, Barry County, Missouri

Husband of Sarah E. (Hagler) Goodnight (Marr. Feb. 16, 1873).

Son of John Henry Jr. & Mary Ann (Stockton) Goodnight.
Preacher and member of Merl's Chapel.

Virgil R. Greenway
Birth:
Mar. 4, 1906
Missouri
Death:

Mar. 27, 1993
Joplin,
Jasper County, Missouri
Burial:
Leann Cemetery,
Leann, Barry County, Missouri,
Plot: Row 30, Plot 419

Early Free Will Baptist preacher in the state of Missouri serving mostly in the region around Monett and southeast Missouri.

Rev J. S. Handyside
Birth:
Aug. 13, 1853
Death:
Mar. 2, 1920
Burial:
McBride Cemetery
Competition
Laclede County
Missouri

Rev. John S. Handyside, was ordained to Freewill Baptist ministry in Missouri, in 1885, having served with the Methodists before.

Archibald Millard Halford
Birth:
Feb. 29, 1888
Dora
Ozark County
Missouri
Death:
Dec. 10, 1961
Norwood
Wright County
Missouri
Burial:
Brushy Knob Cemetery
Vera Cruz
Douglas County
Missouri

SPRINGFIELD DAILY NEWS
Springfield, Greene Co., MO
Wednesday, 13 December 1961

The Rev. Archie M. Halford, 73, of Norwood, died in his home.

He was a minister of the Freewill Baptist Church and had lived in Norwood seven years. He was a native of Douglas County.

Survivors are a brother Thomas C. Halford, Norwood; a stepson Kenneth Pennington, and a stepdaughter Mrs. Hollace Oxley, Mountain Grove; four step-grandchildren and three step-great-grandchildren. Spouse: Ethel Margaret Anderson Halford (1895 - 1961)*

Freddie Dale Harris
BIRTH
1 Jul 1938
Purdy, Barry County, Missouri
DEATH   11 Apr 2016
Purdy, Barry County, Missouri,

BURIAL   Purdy Cemetery
Purdy, Barry County, Missouri,

1956 graduate of Purdy High School. Lifelong resident of Purdy 29 Apr 1961 wed Beverly Jean Adams. Owner operator of Fred Harris Trucking. Pastored in Washburn, Purdy, & Merle's Chapel. Enjoyed fishing, & restoring old cars.

Charles M Hatfield
BIRTH
25 Apr 1898
DEATH
21 Jan 1986 (aged 87)
BURIAL
Sarcoxie Cemetery
Sarcoxie, Jasper County, Missouri,

Pastor of Merl's Chapel 1944-46

Benjamin F Henderson
Birth:
1874
Death:
1950
Burial:
Bethel Cemetery, Monett,
Barry County, Missouri

Early Free Will Baptist preacher in southwestern Missouri.

George Washington Henderson
Birth:
Feb. 17, 1840
Death:
Nov. 10, 1919

Burial:
Shiloh Cemetery
Shook
Wayne County
Missouri

Minister of the Free Will Baptist church, as was his son, James W.M.Henderson.

Rev James Woodrow Monroe Henderson
Birth:
Dec. 30, 1878
Bonne Terre
St. Francois County, Missouri
Death:
Dec. 2, 1944
St. Louis County, Missouri
Burial:
Big River Cemetery
Irondale
Washington County, Missouri

Rev. James W. M. Henderson, was converted in 1919 at the Free Will Baptist Church at Cherryville, St. Francois Co, and was a member of Fredericktown FWB church in Madison Co. It was said that he learned how to read and write by studying the Bible. He was also a pastor of a Mission on South Broadway in St. Louis. He and his wife were injured, he seriously, enroute to church. His wife, Martha/Mattie, suffered a broken wrist, but he died shortly after the accident. Martha lived to age 95 yrs. She is bur. next to her husband in this cemetery."

--from "Henderson History of Southeast Missouri," by E.M. Carroll.

Rev G. W. Hensley
Birth:
1840
Death:
1932
Burial:
Fletchall Cemetery
Grant City, Worth County, Missouri

He represented the Northwest Missouri Yearly Meeting at the Co-operative General Assn of Freewill

Baptists in Plattsburg, Missouri December 1916.

William C Hill
Birth:
Jul. 22, 1920
Death:
Jul. 8, 1986
Burial:
Polk Memorial Cemetery
Ellington
Reynolds County, Missouri:
He served as pastor of the Flat Woods Free Will Baptist Church in St. Francois QM.

Elmer Hodges
Birth:
May 7, 1883
Alton,
Oregon County, Missouri
Death:
Sep. 19, 1960
Alton,
Oregon County, Missouri
Burial:
Smyrna Cemetery, Alton,
Oregon County, Missouri

He was a pastor and minister in southcentral Missouri serving in the early days of the denomination in that region.

Death:
Jun. 21, 1936
Webster County, Missouri
Burial:
Saint Luke Methodist Church
Cemetery
Marshfield, Webster County
Missouri

John Hodges
Birth:
February 12, 1946
Saginaw, Michigan
Death:
October 4, 2019
Springfield, Missouri
Burial:
Rivermonte Memorial Gardens,
Springfield, Missouri

James W Housley
Birth:
1855
Death
: 1937
Burial:
Oak Grove Cemetery
Norwood
Wright County
Missouri

Spouse:
Rebecca Butcher Housley
(1855 - 1912)

John was born to Brice in Florence Murphy Hodges. He graduated from Niangua high school in 1965 and after his graduation he held many positions in the stainless-steel industry. He was called to preach to the ministry in 1973 and pastored several free will Baptist churches in the area.

Rev James T. Holcomb
Birth:
Sep. 23, 1849

King David Hudgens
Birth:
Sep. 16, 1847
Phipps County, Missouri
Death:
Jul. 16, 1920
Burial:
Dunkard Cemetery
Saint Robert

Pulaski County, Missouri

He entered the ministry among the Presbyterians in 1875 and a few years later became a Free Will Baptist with the Big Creek Quarterly Meeting, Prosperity Assn, Missouri ministering to the Liberal church.

Truman Huffman
Birth:
Feb. 2, 1922
Death:
Oct. 26, 2006
Fredericktown
Madison County
Missouri
Burial:
Twin Oak Cemetery
Madison County
Missouri

Rev George Henry Huffman
Birth:
Feb. 26, 1913
Buckhorn
Madison County
Missouri
Death:
Sep. 24, 2001
Farmington
St. Francois County
Missouri
Burial:
Huffman-McKelvey Cemetery
Buckhorn
Madison County
Missouri

Parents: William Pink Huffman (1883 - 1966) - Cora E Stroup Huffman (1884 - 1968)
Spouse: Ruby Alma Gipson Huffman (1912 - 2005)

Spouse: Amy Lee Huffman (1923 - 2006) Children: Judy Huffman Latham (1957 - 2009)

Rev Elihu H. Hunt
Birth:
1814
Burial:
Boyd Cemetery
Holt County
Missouri
Death: 1890
Burial:
Boyd Cemetery
Holt County
Missouri

His name and title(s) are shown in old records where he was a great help to other prominent ministers as they organized churches--i.e. Rev's John and Jeremiah Wood, O.S. Harding, W. H. Copas, and probably others. Note: Rev. E.H. Hunt was a M.D.

Will Baptist Church. She was a member of Professional Women, Chaplain of AARP and the Western Missouri Medical Center

E. Marie Hyatt
Birth:
1920
Death:
April 1, 2002
Burial:
Warrensburg Memorial Gardens Cemetery, Warrensburg, Johnson County, Missouri, Plot: Section 2 Lot 147 Space 1

Rev. E. Marie Hyatt, and Myron E. Hyatt were married at the Free Will Baptist Church, Monett. She served 40 years in church ministry, with the first 12 years with the Free

Lloyd T. Jeffrey's
Birth:
Apr. 23, 1917
Death:
Mar. 4, 1972
Burial:
Monett IOOF Cemetery, Monett, Lawrence County, Missouri

He was a retired Army officer and pastored in the Indian River Association of Free Will Baptist in Southwest Missouri. His wife was the Rev. Opal Jeffrey's and they both pastored Merl's Chapel Free Will Baptist Church near Cassville.

Opal Ethel McClerren Jeffrey's
Birth:
Jul. 8, 1921
Death:
Oct. 2, 2000
Burial:
Monett IOOF Cemetery,
Monett,
Lawrence County, Missouri

She was a well-known Free Will Baptist minister and pastor in southwest Missouri serving for many years the Merl's Chapel Free Will Baptist Church near Cassville. She was married to the Rev. Lloyd Jeffrey's a retired Army officer. A minister's reward is out of this world!

Rev Harry S Johns
Birth:
Jul. 30, 1901
Missouri
Death:
Jul. 1, 1976
Springfield
Greene County,
Burial:
Ragsdale-Harmony Baptist
Cemetery
Seymour
Webster County,
Missouri

Harry is the son of Alexander and Louvada Johns.
He married Beulah Francis Miller on December 20,1930 in Webster County, Missouri.
Four known children were born to this union: Arthur Doyle Johns Lawrence David Johns, Marvin G. Johns Ralph Johns

Rev Bill Jones

Birth:
Sep. 30, 1929
Grove spring
Wright County, Missouri
Death
Mar. 12, 2016
Lebanon
Laclede County, Missouri
Burial:
McBride Cemetery
Competition
Laclede County, Missouri

Brother Jones was born to George Ralph and Opal Estelle Jones. On February 10, 1950, he married Wilma McClanahan and they were married for 66 years at the time of his passing.

He served in the United States Army and pastored the Pleasant view Free Will Baptist Church, Little Vine Free Will Baptist church, Cope, Happy Hill and Liberty Free Will Baptist churches. He was also employed with Ben Stephen construction, ran heavy equipment and loved farming and raising cattle. His services were officiated by Dan Talbot, Craig Perry and R. E. Helsley.

Arthur A. Kicenski

Birth:
Dec. 21, 1896
Death:
Dec. 29, 1970
Burial:
Clintonville Cemetery,
El Dorado Springs,
Cedar County,
Missouri

He was active Free Will Baptist minister serving in the Missouri & Kansas region.

John Gilbert Koch

Birth:
Nov. 25, 1869
Death:
Sep. 27, 1952
Burial:
White Rock Cemetery
Texas County
Missouri

Early minister in Union Assn.
Parents:
Julius Koch (1833 - 1918)
Dialtha Pryor Koch (1840 - 1902)
Spouse:
Matilda Lou Daily Koch (1882 - 1953)*

Levi Theodore Koch
Birth:
Mar. 12, 1879
Death:
Aug. 6, 1947
Burial:
White Rock Cemetery
Texas County
Missouri

SFC 301 Wagon Co QMC WWI
Family links: Parents:
 Julius Koch (1833 - 1918)
 Dialtha Pryor Koch (1840 - 1902)
Siblings:
 John Gilbert Koch (1869 - 1952)
 Rhoda Koch (1871 - 1943)
 Dora Elizabeth Koch (
1873 - 1943)
 Christian Julius Koch
(1877 - 1961)
 Levi Throdore Koch
(1879 - 1947)

Absalom Sussdorf Lick
Birth:
Jul. 31, 1853
Illinois
Death:

Jul. 17, 1942
Springfield,
Greene County, Missouri
Burial:
Dixon Cemetery, Dixon,
Pulaski County, Missouri

He served in central Missouri.

Rev Julius Arthur LeRoux
Birth:
Sep. 9, 1841
Paris, France
Death:
Mar. 25, 1931
Doniphan
Ripley County
Missouri
Burial:
Oak Grove Cemetery
Ripley County, Missouri

George Million in his history of this area said "No man can jump higher, turn around quicker, squall louder, of get happier than Elder Leroux.

Before joining the General Free Will Baptists, he had been a preacher in the Missionary Baptists. He was ordained in 1884. He was of French extraction, a good man, tireless worker and few men did more for the advancement of the cause than he. He was a great revivalist. He went with the General Baptists later. He was married to Matilda Margaret Pennington LeRoux (1849 - 1911) and Margaret Louise Barnes LeRoux (1855 - 1948).

Inscription:
CPL CO D 188 OHIO INF CIVIL WAR

Rev Sylvester Bowman Lewis
Birth:
Mar. 22, 1846
Death:
May 23, 1921
Burial:
Muddy Cemetery
Pattonsburg, Daviess County
Missouri

Rev. S. B. Lewis was an ordained Free Will Baptist minister/pastor in Missouri. He was in the early Missouri state work. In 1917, he was in attendance at the organization of the Cooperative General Association of churches and districts, (that did not go into the 1911 merger of the northern Free Will Baptists), held at the Philadelphia Church, Davies Co. MO., evidenced by his name appearing in the roster of ordained ministers present. He stated his home was Pattonsburg, MO. He was in Missouri State ministers list of Freewill Baptist in 1896.

Rev Claude V Lincoln
Birth:
Nov. 1, 1887
Mine La Motte
Madison County,
Missouri
Death:
Mar. 12, 1942
Esther
St. Francois County, Missouri
Burial:
Parkview Cemetery
Farmington
St. Francois County,
Missouri

Claude Lincoln passed away at his home in Esther after an illness of nearly two years with tuberculosis. His name is in the Hist. of Flat River FWB Church as then (1938) pastor in St. Louis church. Funeral services were held by Rev. James Miller of North Missouri, a former pastor of the church, assisted by Rev. Cecil Campbell, evangelist who is conducting revival services at the church. Mr. Lincoln had worked for the St. Joseph Lead Co. for the past 23 years.

He was converted when a young man and united with the Free Will Baptist Church at Mine La Motte, but had been a member of the Flat River Church for the past 21 years.

Rev John David Long
Birth:
Feb. 3, 1899
Death:
Jul. 25, 1976
Saint Louis
St. Louis City
Missouri
Burial:
Marcus Memorial Cemetery
Fredericktown
Madison County

Missouri pastor who spent most of his life in southeast Missouri, was pastor of the Parkview FWB church after Lizzie McAdams held a meeting in the former Second Missionary Baptist Church of Desloge changing their affiliation to Free Will Baptists. He was a leading minister in the St. François conference.

Rev Russell M Lowe
Birth
21 Nov 1942
Death
9 Sep 2017
McAlester, Pittsburg County, Oklahoma,
Burial
Saint Marys Cemetery
Saint Mary, Ste. Genevieve County, Missouri,

Born to Gladys Ford Lowe and James Vincent Lowe. Russell lived his life in Clyde, North Carolina until he graduated from high school in 1961. He enlisted immediately in the U.S. Air Force where he served our country until 1965. He met Gracie Jane Hannah and on June 2, 1966 they were married and started their life together. They moved to Michigan that fall and that is where he came in contact with the gospel. His mother-in-law, Ruby and father-in-law, Paul, never failed to invite them to church and on Christmas of 1972, where Russell met the Lord and gave his heart to Him. Gracie rededicated her life that same day. This is where Russell became a soldier of the cross because, from the very first day he told everyone what the Lord did for him. When he went back into the car plant, where he worked they knew something had happened to him. He drove a Cushman truck to deliver parts and they nicknamed him the Holy Ghost express. It didn't upset him, it just made him smile. He surrendered to preach in October of 1973 and was ordained in November 1975 in Wayne, Michigan. He has served as Pastor in Church's in Michigan, West Virginia, Idaho (National Home Missionary), and last 29 years in Oklahoma. He attended Nashville Free Will Baptist Bible College, Degree Graduate of Theology and Bachelor of Religious Education from Trinity College in Newburgh, Indiana in 1991, Master of Theology from Andersonville Baptist Seminary in Camelia, Georgia in 1996, and Doctor of Theology with honors, Andersonville Baptist Seminary in 2010. He always said, "I just want to be the best that I can be for the Lord who gave His all for me!". He loved his Lord, his wife, his family,

God's people and the lost. He was preceded in death by his mother, Gladys Lowe, father, Vincent Lowe, a brother, John David Lowe and a sister, Judith Ann Lowe. His Going Home Celebration was held at the First Free Will Baptist Church on Carl Albert Parkway in McAlester, Oklahoma.

Cora Ann Hamilton Mann
Birth:
Jun. 8, 1875
Schuyler County, Missouri
Death
Sep. 9, 1934
Schuyler County, Missouri
Burial:
Jimtown Cemetery
Queen City
Schuyler County, Missouri

She was a minister who represented the Northwest Missouri Yearly Meeting at the Co-operative General Association of Freewill Baptists in Plattsburg, Missouri December 1916. She was the daughter of John L. Hamilton and Addie Grimes. She was the wife of Rev. Charles Earl Mann (1875 - 1943).

Charles Earl Mann
Birth:
Jul. 8, 1875
Glenwood,
Schuyler County, Missouri
Death:
Mar. 20, 1943
Jackson County, Missouri
Burial:
Jimtown Cemetery,
Queen City
Schuyler County, Missouri

He was an early minister and pastor in central Missouri. He was the Clerk of the Missouri State Association and along with his wife represented the Northwest Missouri Yearly Meeting at the Co-operative General Association of Freewill Baptists in Plattsburg, Missouri December 1916. Son of Nathan Mann and Loreda Charlotte. Married (1st) on 4 October 1899 in Schuyler County, Missouri to Cora Ann Hamilton, and (2nd) on 18 December 1937 in Marshfield, Webster County, Missouri to Emaline Hightower (widow of Rev. Marion Benjamin Clift).

Thomas J. Mann
Birth:
1880
Death:
1943
Burial:
Pendleton Cemetery
Doe Run
St. Francois County, Missouri

He was pastor of the church in Flat River in 1918.

Samuel H Marcum
Birth:
Aug. 14, 1891
Death:
Mar. 19, 1975
Burial:
Evergreen Cemetery,
Cameron,
Clinton County, Missouri

An early Minister and active leader in the state of Missouri.
Parents:
William M Marcum (1860 - 1900)

Annalocka Jane Wisdom Marcum (1861 - 1950)- Spouse: Daisy D Marcum Marcum (1900 - 1996)*

Rev Elias Matney
Birth:
Apr. 17, 1871
Death:
Oct. 23, 1950
Burial:
Murray Cemetery
Squires
Douglas County, Missouri

Family links: Parents: Uriah Matney (1834 - 1899)- Catherine Cobb Matney (1837 - 1886)
Spouse: Jane Manning Ecton Matney (1856 - 1938)
Children: John Matney (1891 - 1946); Henry Everett Matney (1892 - 1965);   Ruth J. Matney Hartley (1899 - 1971)

Rev Luke M. Marler, Jr
Birth:
Jun. 15, 1872
Douglas County
Missouri
Death:
Mar. 2, 1958
Missouri
Burial:
Fannon Cemetery
Ava
Douglas County
Missouri

Rev James Franklin McCall
Birth:
Nov. 18, 1857
Illinois
Death:
Jan. 22, 1933
Norwood
Wright County
Missouri
Burial:

Denlow Cemetery
Denlow
Douglas County,
Missouri

Rev. J. F. McCall, 76 years old, passed quietly to his eternal rest at his home in Norwood early Sunday morning. Mrs. McCall had prepared breakfast and when she went to call her husband found him dead.

Short services were conducted at the home here by Rev. G. Chadwell Tuesday morning, after which the body was taken to Denlow for interment, Rev. Halford preaching the funeral sermon there. Rev. McCall has been in failing health for some time. He had spent many years in the ministry of the Freewill Baptist church, being a successful evangelist as well as a faithful pastor of many churches.

Rev Billy "James" McCully
Birth:
May 1, 1925
Neosho, Neton County,
Missouri
Death:
Jan 22, 2008
Monett, Barry County,
Missouri
Burial:
Monett IOOF Cemetery,
Monett, Missouri

James McCully, died at Cox Monett Hospital. He was born in Neosho, the son of Jefferson David and Josephene Odessa (Ball) McCully. He was pastor of Merl's Chapel in Cassville and owned and operated Hometown Outlet. He was former owner of M & M Tire and M & M Sanitation in Monett. He was a member of the First Freewill Baptist Church in Monett and an Army veteran of World War II. He married his wife, Louise, on March 12, 1943, in Monett. - Military Stone - Inscription: "B. JAMES MCCULLY PVT US ARMY WORLD WAR II"

Rev W. L. McClanahan
Birth:
Jan. 30, 1884
Death:
May 5, 1974
Burial:
Eureka Cemetery
Rader
Webster County, Missouri

Evans Boyd McClintock
Birth:
Apr. 27, 1857
Milledgeville
McNairy County, Tennessee
Death:
Nov. 2, 1926
Springfield
Greene County, Missouri
Burial:
Greenlawn Memorial Gardens

Springfield
Greene County, Missouri

Spouse - Mattie T Painer
Father - Alexander H McClintock
(born TN) Mother - Cynthia Evans
(born TN)

Occupation - Retired minister
Info from MO death cert

Billy Gene McClintock
Birth:
Sep. 8, 1932
Doniphan, Missouri
Death:
Sep. 26, 2012
Poplar Bluff Regional Medical
Center
Poplar Bluff, Missouri
Burial:
Johnston Chapel
Ripley County, Missouri

Mr. McClintock, son of Raymond and Fay Ilene (Phillips) McClintock. He had been an auto mechanic and was minister and founder of Lingo Freewill Baptist Church. A minister of the gospel; served in New Mexico in the 1970's. Mr. McClintock enjoyed woodworking and had a special interest in the historical enactment of Ripley County Civil War Days and Timberfest.
On August 1, 1953, he was married to Joyce Marilyn Langlois at Detroit, Michigan. She preceded him in death on December 4, 2003.

John D McKown
Birth:
Apr. 29, 1892
Daviess County, Missouri
Death:
Mar., 1982
Jamesport,
Daviess County,
Missouri
Burial:
Clear Creek Cemetery,
Lock Springs,
Daviess County,
Missouri

Rev William Henry McKown
Birth:
Aug. 2, 1846
Preble County, Ohio
Death:
1926
Daviess County, Missouri
Burial:
Clear Creek Cemetery
Lock Springs
Daviess County, Missouri

His ministry was basically confined to Daviess County Missouri. Note: his life and ministry extended 90 years.

Wm. F. Millard
Birth:
Aug. 18, 1874
Death:
Aug. 15, 1958
Burial:
Lebanon City Cemetery,
Lebanon
Laclede County, Missouri,
Plot: 18-5 Blk 14

An early Free Will Baptist minister in Laclede County Missouri.

Rev Charles L Miller
BIRTH
18 May 1927
Bunker, Reynolds County, Missouri
DEATH
19 May 2019 (aged 92)
Missouri,
BURIAL
Woodlawn Memorial Park
De Soto,
Jefferson County,
Missouri

Born a son to John and Mildred (nee Hall) Miller. He was 92. He is survived by his wife of 73 years Imalea (nee Briley) Miller, De Soto. He is preceded in death by his parents; two sons: John Harvey Miller and Charles "Chuck" Miller. Rev. Miller was the Pastor of Parkview Free Will Baptist Church for 7 years then First Free Will Baptist Church-De Soto for 25 years and also was an Evangelist.

George Miller
Birth:
Sep. 3, 1834

Death:
Jan. 11, 1900
Burial:
Elmwood Cemetery,
Kansas City,
Jackson County,
Missouri

One of the early Free Will Baptist ministers in western Missouri.

James F. Miller

Birth:
Sep. 3, 1894
Bollinger County,
Missouri
Death:
May 14, 1965
Farmington,
St. Francois County, Missouri
Burial:
Union Light Cemetery, Loyd,
Bollinger County, Missouri

During his ministry he pastored in four different states: Missouri, Texas, North Carolina and Tennessee. He was elected the Missouri State Moderator for Free Will Baptists in 1933 where he served eleven years.

He was elected as Moderator of the National Association of Free Will Baptists in 1938, a position he held for seven consecutive years. He served as a member of the Board of Trustees to the Free Will Baptist Bible College for sixteen years. The college yearbook was dedicated to him in 1963. He received a life time honorary membership in the college Alumni Association in April, 1965. He became a representative of the college in his later years and traveled in 16 states in the interest of the school. Funeral service were held at the Farmington Free Will Baptist Church by the Rev. Charles Thigpen, Dean of the college in Nashville, Tennessee. He was assisted by the Rev Everett Hellard, pastor of the church.

Brantly Sigle Moody

Birth:
May 28, 1884
Norwood
Wright County,Missouri
Death:
Jun. 7, 1963
Norwood
Wright County
Missouri
Burial:
Thomas Cemetery
Norwood
Wright County,Missouri
Plot: S-35 #5431

He is the son of Jonathan and Mary Jane (Barnett) Moody. On August 31, 1905 he was united in marriage to Elizabeth Zoella "Lizzie" Caudle. To this union four known children were born.

Family links: Parents: Jonathan Moody (1858 - 1948)
 Mary Jane Barnett Moody (1866 - 1931)
 Spouse: Elizabeth Zoella Caudle Moody (1885 - 1972)*

Glenn Edwin Murray
Birth:
Mar. 10, 1935
Doniphan
Ripley County
Missouri
Death:
Mar. 26, 2016
Hartville
Wright County
Missouri
Burial:
Howell Memorial Park Cemetery
Pomona
Howell County
Missouri

Rev John W Moore
Birth:
1871
Death:
May 24, 1958
Burial:
Odd Fellows Cemetery
Neosho
Newton County
Missouri

Spouse: Anna Pendleton Callahan Moore (1876 - 1955)
Inscription: 87yrs

He was born to Jess Earl Murray and Clara Marie Crook Murray. He graduated from Doniphan High School with the Class of 1953. Reverend Murray was a veteran, having served with the United States National Guard. On September 24, 1955, he was married at West Plains, Missouri, to Rachel Victoria Adkisson. He worked at sawmills and restored antique furniture; having worked at Joplin Brothers Handle Factory and Smith Gas Company. While working at Cloud Oak Flooring, he answered the call to preach; he ministered for the next fifty-five years. On December 11, 1960 he preached his first sermon at the First Freewill Baptist Church, West Plains and where he was later ordained to preach on April 2, 1962 when his son, Jon, was ten days old. Susie Murray Stillwell was the first convert, at the Oak Grove Church of God, Doniphan, Missouri on January 1, 1961. He preached 9,700 sermons, saved 2,370 souls, officiated 1,900 funerals, 200 weddings, 700 baptisms and preached at over 700 revivals. Reverend Murray served at Pleasant Home Freewill Baptist Church, Alton Freewill Baptist Church, Hannon Freewill Baptist Church, Cabool Freewill Baptist Church, Oak Grove Church of God, First Freewill Baptist Church, Batesville, Arkansas, United Freewill Baptist Church, West Plains, State Line, Victory (Myrtle), Dry Creek and Hartville. He enjoyed turkey hunting, taking his 100th in the spring of 2015.

Jesse Niswonger
Birth:
Apr. 6, 1848, Millersville
Cape Girardeau County
Missouri
Death: Jul. 5, 1935
Cape Girardeau
Cape Girardeau County
Missouri
Burial:
Niswonger Cemetery
(Near Fruitland)
Cape Girardeau County
Missouri

Son of Joseph NISWONGER and Susana HAHS. Early FWB minister n the General Free Will Baptist Conference.

John H Noble

Birth:
Jun. 24, 1832
McMinn County, Tennessee
Death:
Jul. 13, 1903
Burial:
Ashland Cemetery
Saint Joseph
Buchanan County, Missouri

In 1861 he married Betty Tuck. His conversion took place in 1866 and ordination in 1872. He united with the Free Baptists in 1876 and has conducted several revivals and organized four churches. Besides pastorates in Tennessee he also pastored in Missouri where he died.

Benjamin Melton Owens

Birth:
Feb. 28, 1886
Norwood
Wright County
Missouri
Death:
Oct. 26, 1969
Mountain Grove
Wright County
Missouri
Burial:
Hopewell Cemetery
Texas County,Missouri

Family links: Parents: Isaac Owens (1855 - 1939) - Sarah Catherine Bradshaw Owens (1852 - 1937)
Spouses:
Arizona Cartwright Owens (1889 - 1960)

Parlee Jane Reece Souder (1877 - 1970)*
Children:
Florence Owens Ratteree (1910 - 1984)*
Joseph Morris Owens (1918 - 1996)*
Fern Ratterree (1920 - 1991)*
Elijah M Owens (1928 - 1999)

James Coy Powell

Birth:
Dec. 25, 1923
Dunklin County,
Missouri

Death:
Jan. 4, 1994
Flint
Genesee County, Michigan
Burial:
Mount Gilead Cemetery
Clarkton
Dunklin County, Missouri

His parents were Colombus Powell, and Luella Powell. He was one of several children. He married Sally Jane McFarland 8 Feb. 1943, in St. Louis, MO. A Free Will Baptist minister. He was pastor of the Friendship FWB in Flint, Michigan for many years.

John Postlewaite
Birth:
Apr. 5, 1926
Graff, Missouri.
Death:
Oct. 21, 2012
Sentera Leigh Hospital
Norfolk, Virginia
Burial:
Hillcrest Cemetery
Mountain Grove, Wright County,
Missouri

He was the 8th son of the late John Jefferson and Lucy Jane (Crewse) Postlewaite. He was 86 years, 6 months, and 16 days of age at his death.John was saved at the age of 12 at the No. 1 Free Will Baptist Church near Huggins, Missouri, when his teacher dismissed school for the students to attend an 11:00 revival service. He answered the call to preach at the age of 19. After attending Free Will Baptist Bible College (now Welch College) in Nashville, Tennessee, he was ordained as a minister of the gospel in 1947. He married Leah Mae Scott on September 21, 1948 at the home of Rev. Homer B. Smith near Mountain Grove. To this union were born 4 children. John's first pastorate was at Faith and Hope Free Will Baptist Church near Willow Springs, Missouri. There John and Leah lived in a small log cabin, which was the church parsonage. Throughout the next 53 years, he pastored churches in Oklahoma, Arkansas, Illinois, and Missouri. He planted 7 churches in Washington and Oregon under the auspices of Free Will Baptist Home Missions. He was a well-known evangelist, soul winner, supporter of missions, and mentor to many young people. After moving back to Mountain Grove in his retirement years, he served as Senior Citizens' Pastor at First Free Will Baptist for almost 8 years. He had a lovely tenor voice and often sang in church and at home. He was also a lover of the Scripture and committed many passages to memory. Even in his last days, he spent several hours a day reading the Bible and could still quote many passages. He and his wife, Leah, shared 64 years. His four children were: Joe and Pauline Postlewaite of Florence, South Carolina; Sue and Earl Larson of Brentwood, Tennessee; Sam and Diana Postlewaite of Virginia Beach, Virginia; and Ruth and Donnie McDonald of Tokyo, Japan. Only eternity will reveal how many spiritual children were saved because of his faithful witness

John Learner Ratteree
Birth:
Sep. 11, 1885
Death:
Apr. 8, 1962
Burial:
Hopewell Cemetery
Texas County
Missouri

Early minister in Union Assn. John was the son of David and Manerva Zirschky Ratterree. He married

Florence Owens on February 24, 1929. This union 7 children were born. He was ordained as a minister in 1926. He was of the Free Will Baptist faith.

William T. 'Bill' Reeves
Birth:
Jan. 1, 1902
Death:
Sep. 15, 1994
Burial:
Big River Cemetery, Irondale, Washington County, Missouri

He ministered in central Missouri and was a regular contributor to the Free Will Baptist Gem. An influential officer and leader in the state Sunday school convention. In later years he was superintendent of the youth camp at Niangua which continues today as a beautiful and well attended camp for Missouri youth.

Elder Samuel Nelson Reid
Birth:
1868
Death:
1946
Burial:
Crossroads Cemetery,
Lebanon,
Laclede County, Missouri

He was an early pastor and minister in the central region of the state of Missouri.

William Haye Revelle
Birth:
Apr., 1845
Death:
Dec. 4, 1916
Burial:
Revelle Cemetery (Ebenezer)
Cherokee Pass
Madison County, Missouri
He was an early preacher in the
General Free Will Baptist Assn. The
son of Jackson and Cordelia
(Lincoln) Revelle.

Arthur Leroy Rich
Birth:
Aug. 22, 1883
Wright County, Missouri
Death:
Feb. 26, 1969
Wright County, Missouri
Burial:
Ashley Cemetery
Wright County, Missouri

Family links: Parents: Robert
Thomas Rich (1842 - 1918)
Spouse: Arbella Moody Rich
(1889 - 1968)
Children: Dora Ione Rich Smith
(1918 - 2014), Charles Clinton Rich
(1920 - 1990)

The Divine Power Appears Fearful In Its Holiness

John Byron Rollins
Birth:
Jul. 16, 1912
Stone County, Missouri
Death:
Jul. 6, 2003
Jefferson City,
Cole County, Missouri
Burial:
Hawthorn Memorial Gardens,
Jefferson City,
Cole County, Missouri

Dee Roy Royster
Birth:
Jan. 6, 1892
Competition
Laclede County, Missouri
Death:
May 3, 1935
Wright County, Missouri
Burial:
Coldwater Cemetery
Manes
Wright County, Missouri

He was a 1932 graduate of Purdy High School in Purdy, Missouri. He was a Free Will Baptist minister who as early Minister and pastor began work with the Free Will Baptist GEM as a printer and writer.

When the founder B. F. Brown retired at age 70, he was succeeded by Rev. Rollins. In this position he traveled much of the State of Missouri.

He was a prolific writer, theologian, and well respected by his peers. He moved to Jefferson City where he united with the Southern Baptist, serving the Russellville Baptist Church, New Hope Baptist Church, Elston Baptist Church, Enon Baptist Church, Cole Springs Baptist Church, and the Little Flock Baptist Church in Vienna. He began to work with the *Word and Way* newspaper for the Missouri Baptist and by the time of his death at age 90 had performed 1648 weddings in the Jefferson City area.

Source: History and Families of Wright County, Missouri, 1841-1991, page 529. ROYSTER - Dee Royster (Jan. 6, 1892, near Competition, MO) was the son of Sam and Laura Bohannon Royster. In 1902, his mother died of typhoid fever leaving six children, the youngest five months old. This sad experience never left Dee's mind and he often told his children to respect their mother at all times.

On March 17, 1914, he married Grace Wynn (March 14, 1895 near St. George, MO) daughter of John and Elmire Duncan Wynn. John owned three farms and Dee and Grace lived on one of them while Dee farmed John's land. While living in the St. George and Manes area Dee and Grace had two children: Norman (Sept. 5, 1915) and Erma (Feb. 25, 1917). Norman died of Pneumonia when one month old. The parents could never understand the "Why" but knew God always knows best.

In 1919 Dee and Grace lived in Idaho working to obtain extra money to buy their farm. In 1922, they bought a farm located near Grimes Mill on the Gasconade River. Two years later a son Doyle was born on May 5, 1924.

Dee Royster was a very prosperous farmer and soon had his farm in excellent condition. When moving to this community, the family searched for a church of their choice and found it at Coon Creek Free Will Baptist Church. It was four miles from them which was quite a distance to travel in a buggy, but foul weather did not keep them from church. It was in that church that Dee preached his first sermon on July 7, 1924. He was the type of person that everyone he came in contact with knew him on a first name basis. That was quite an asset in his ministry. He would leave early on a Saturday morning to ride horseback many miles to the churches he pastored. That left his wife to care for the two children and do many farm chores, but she never complained. The family believed in always putting the Lord first. Riding so far in low temperatures, Dee must have suffered with the cold, but he never mentioned preaching being

any hardship. In 1928, he bought a new Model A Ford car which kept him from enduring the cold going to the churches he pastored; but the roads were rough and the streams unbridged so trips by car were not always without unpleasant events. In 1935, he bought a new Ford V8 pickup, but he only drove it a few times to the churches he pastored. He was never very well, but he did not complain. His life ended on May 3, 1935 when he died from complications of an ear infection following the flu. His funeral at the Cope Church, was attended by the largest crowd which had ever assembled there.

Grace remained on the farm until 1962. She then sold it and bought a house in Mt. Grove where she lived until she had a fatal heart attack March 19, 1981.

John F. Schebaum
Birth:
Aug. 7, 1918
Death:
Jul. 7, 2000

Burial:
Big Creek Cemetery
Yukon
Texas County, Missouri

He was converted in 1955 and was ordained as a Deacon before answering his called to preach in 1963.

During his 37 years of ministry he pastored six Free Will Baptist churches in Missouri and one in Tennessee. He also served as a supply pastor for several churches and maintained an active tape ministry and Bible study at two nursing homes. At the time of his passing he was a member of the First Free Will Baptist Church in Waynesville, Missouri. He was married to Lorene Emeline Dixon Schebaum (1918 - 2011).

George Washington Scott
Birth:
Jun. 28, 1865
Ozark County, Missouri
Death:
Dec. 30, 1960
Wright County, Missouri

Burial:
Mountain Valley Cemetery,
Mountain Grove,
Wright County, Missouri

He pastored several churches in the area.

Rev George William Scott
BIRTH
18 Dec 1890
Huggins, Texas County, Missouri,
DEATH
7 Mar 1957 (aged 66)
Springfield, Greene County,
Missouri, USA
BURIAL
Hillcrest Cemetery
Mountain Grove, Wright County,
Missouri, USA
PLOT   SE 1st 29-5

George was the son of Foster Flemon and Nancy Howe Wilson Scott. He married Oma Lucinda Tanny Ratterree on September 21, 1910. To this union 10 children were born.

James W Sellards
Birth:
Jun. 28, 1835
Floyd County, Kentucky
Death:
Aug. 8, 1897
Missouri
Burial:
Barber-Whitener Cemetery
Zion
Madison County, Missouri

He was brought to God in 1861, and ordained by the larger Baptist body in 1864 laboring with them in Minnesota. He experienced much difficulty because of his open communion views; and, on moving to Missouri and learning of the Free Baptists at Fredericktown in 1885 where he united with the church.

Rev John Wesley Silvey
Birth:
Sep. 5, 1874
Clay County
Missouri
Death:
Mar. 8, 1954
Douglas County
Missouri
Burial:
Fannon Cemetery
Ava
Douglas County
Missouri

Per death certificate, parents Melvin Silvey and Mary Wolf, spouse. 1910-1930 Spring Creek, Douglas, MO.
Children: Lilith, Mabel E, Raleigh E, John L, Roy L, Melvin G, Lois F, Beulah C.

Elza Elisha Simpson
Birth:
Dec. 13, 1898
Wilderness,
Oregon County, Missouri
Death:
Sep. 25, 1994
St. Louis County,
Missouri
Burial:
Smyrna Cemetery, Alton,

Oregon County,
Missouri

Richard 'Milo' Standley
Birth:
Jun. 14, 1859
Pennsylvania
Death:
Dec. 31, 1935
Couch, Oregon County,Missouri
Burial:
New Salem Cemetery,
Couch, Oregon County,
Missouri

Son of William Richard Standley and Mary (Mathias) Standley. He first married Virgiline Crowell (1869-1932) on 07-Sep-1884 at Oregon Co., MO. Afterwards he married Caroline Mary Harder (1860-1892) about 1894. He was a farmer and preacher. Standley, of Cave Springs Association, gave his life for the cause of Christ. He traveled many miles in a buggy, pulled by a white mule named Maude. He preached in the Missouri and Arkansas Lapland: Many Springs, Walnut Grove, Bonds, New Salem, Hideout School House, Corning and Paragould, Arkansas, to name a few. Many were saved and baptized under his preaching. He and his wife, Caroline Harder, foster daughter to Judge John F. Harder of Many Springs, lived at Couch, Missouri.

William Preston Stogsdill
Birth:
Jan. 31, 1870
Oregon County, Missouri
Death:
Jul. 18, 1944
Oregon County, Missouri
Burial:
Cave Springs Cemetery,
Alton, Oregon County, Missouri
Free Will Baptist minister in south central Missouri.

John C Swaffar
Birth:
Jun. 19, 1904
Death:
May 31, 1996
Burial:
New Site Cemetery, Monett,
Barry County, Missouri

Minister in South west Missouri

John H Tally
Birth:
Dec. 25, 1878
Ash Flat,
Sharp County, Arkansas
Death:
Aug. 22, 1948 Thayer, Oregon
County,
Missouri
Burial:
Walker Cemetery,

Thayer,
Oregon County, Missouri

Ministry was mainly in southern Missouri.

Grover V Terry
Birth:
Apr. 7, 1913
Death:
Sep. 8, 1999
Burial:
Marshfield Cemetery
Marshfield Webster County,
Missouri

One of the leading Missouri pastors and very active in denominational affairs prior to his retirement.

Roena Cassatt Thomas
Birth:
1898
Death:
1959
Burial:
Worsley Cemetery,
Bronaugh,
Vernon County, Missouri

She was a Free Will Baptist Minister for 26 years in the state of Missouri.

Inscription:
Minister -
26 years

Lawrence Delmon Thompson
Birth:
May 16, 1925
Salem, Dent County, Missouri
Death:
Sep. 17, 1980
Saint Louis, St. Louis County,
Missouri
Burial:
Salem Grove Cemetery, Salem
Dent County, Missouri

Lawrence Thompson was a WWII Navy Vet, and was a pastor for 28 years. He was killed in a light plane crash along with 2 other pastors from the St. Louis area. He is remembered for his strong leadership in the state of Missouri.

Kenneth Turner
Birth:
Nov. 27, 1907
Death:
Feb. 8, 1998
Burial:
Jones Chapel Cemetery,
Stella,
Newton County, Missouri

Minister, pastor, and able denominational leader. He pastored churches in Missouri, Arkansas, Oklahoma and Kansas. He was on a Joplin TV station doing magic acts in the middle 50's. He went to Cuba three times filming the mission work there and traveled for 15 years in the United States raising funds for foreign missions. He served five years as president of the Free Will Baptist League and served in numerous roles in denominational offices during his 66 years of ministry.

Rev Clarence Ussery
Birth:
Mar. 25, 1896
Norwood
Wright County
Missouri
Death:
May 9, 1949

Missouri
Burial:
Oak Grove Cemetery
Norwood
Wright County
Missouri

Clarence Ussery, son of Jospeh & Margaret (Tudors) Ussery, His age was 53 years, 1 month, 14 days. He was reared and educated in Blanchard School district, five miles north of Norwood, MO.

He was united in marriage to Cleo Lathrom on December 10, 1916. To this union five children were born.

He was united in marriage to Minnie Florence Adams on September 9, 1930. To this union was born two children.

Clarence professed faith in Christ on October 23,1916, and united with the Oak Grove Freewill Baptist Church where he remained a faithful member until his death. He was ordained as minister of the Gospel by the Union Association of Freewill Baptist at Pleasant Hill Church on august 30, 1918. He did pastorial work and conducted many revival meetings in Missouri and neighboring states for 31 years. It was his pleasure to witness many conversions. When he was called to rest, he was the pastor of the Freewill Baptist Church #1 near Huggins MO and Willow Springs Church #2 near Vanzant MO.

Services were held at Oak Grove with Rev Oliver Letterman and Rev Verle Tate officiating.

Herbert Steaven Vandivort
Birth:
May 20, 1909
Texas County
Missouri
Death:
Nov. 16, 2002
Phelps County
Missouri
Burial:
Hillcrest Cemetery
Mountain Grove
Wright County
Missouri
Plot: S.E. 1st 76-6

Herbert Steaven Hadley was the son of William Warren and Rosa Bell Meadows Vandivort. He married Bessie Jane Scott on February 28, 1934. To this union 3 sons were born. He became a ordained Free Will Baptist minister Sept. 27, 1935. For 21 years from 1937 to 1958, he served as a bi-vocational minister, pastoring rural churches in Texas and Wright counties.

Robert J Warner
Birth:
Mar. 16, 1941
Death:
Feb. 15, 1997
Fredericktown,
Madison County,
Missouri
Burial:
Mine La Motte Cemetery,
Mine La Motte,
Madison County,
Missouri

A minister, and denominational officer. He retired after 20 years in the military and returned to Missouri where he farmed and pastored. He was the Clerk of the Missouri State Association at the time of his death.

"Jesus Christ is in the noblest, and most perfect sense, the realized ideal of humanity."

Ira Waterman
Birth:
Nov. 6, 1873
Missouri
Death:
Nov. 23, 1926
Laclede County, Missouri
Burial
Hufft Cemetery
Eldridge, Laclede County, Missouri

Free Will Baptist minister, evangelist and public school teacher. He was very active in the early stages of the Missouri State Association.

Mary Elizabeth *Retherford*
Wellbaum
Birth:
1887
Death:
1972
Burial:
Greentop Cemetery, Greentop,
Schuyler County, Missouri
She was a well-known and respected Free Will Baptist minister in central Missouri.

Lemuel W Waterman
Birth:
Dec. 25, 1883
Death:
Feb. 22, 1968
Burial:
Hufft Cemetery
Eldridge
Laclede County
Missouri

Willie K. Weston
Birth:
Sep. 30, 1904
Death:

Apr. 9, 1988
Burial:
Monett IOOF Cemetery,
Monett,
Lawrence County, Missouri

He was a well-known pastor and minister in Indian Association in southwestern Missouri and was a regular contributor to the Free Will Baptist GEM.

Rev Marion Henry Williams
Birth:
Jun. 11, 1869
Wright County, Missouri
Death:
Jun. 22, 1947
Wright County
Missouri
Burial:
Davis Cemetery
Wright County,
Missouri,

Marion Henry Williams was the son of Henry McKinley Williams and Amanda Margaret Stevenson. He married Alcey Ellen Williams. He was a Free Will Baptist minister.

Paul Williams
Birth:
Feb. 9, 1918
Carterville,
Jasper County, Missouri
Death:
Jan. 12, 1963
Duquesne,
Jasper County, Missouri
Burial:
Carterville Cemetery,
Carterville,
Jasper County, Missouri,
Plot: Section 4A, Lot 48

He founded the Joplin Free Will Baptist Church where he served for eight years before an unexpected heart attack. Prior to this he pastored the Carterville Free Will Baptist Church. He was an active member of the Joplin Ministerial Alliance and the Niangua Youth Camp Board. He was also an officer on the State Executive Board and the Indian Creek Association Executive Board.

over one hundred converts. His labors have been in the St. Francois County, Mo., Q. M. which is the oldest in the state of Missouri. The results of his earlier work is still existent in that area.

Jeremiah Wood
Birth:
Apr. 24, 1824
Virginia
Death:
Jan. 9, 1913
Doe Run,
St. Francois County, Missouri
Burial:
Doe Run Memorial Cemetery,
Doe Run,
St. Francois County, Missouri

Rev. Jeremiah, brother of Rev. John Wood, was born in Randolph County, Va. He was converted in 1847, was licensed to preach by the United Brethren in 1868, and ordained by the Freewill Baptists the next year. He assisted in organizing four churches, baptizing

Joshua Wood, Jr
Birth:
Apr. 12, 1857
Meigs County, Ohio
Death:
Jan. 11, 1928
St. Francois County, Missouri
Burial:
Cedar Falls Cemetery, Desloge,
St. Francois County, Missouri

He received license to preach Dec. 25, 1885. He has been for several years a student at Carleton Institute, Farmington, Mo., and was clerk of the St. Francois County Q. M. He is a part of the early Wood families that migrated to this part of Missouri from Ohio who were founders of the oldest existing quarterly meeting in Missouri.

his conversion, which took place in 1853. In 1871 he received license to preach, and three years later he was ordained. He has since engaged in revival and pastoral work. His labors have been largely instrumental in building up the St. Francois County Q. M., Missouri, all the churches of which, except two, he has either organized or assisted in organizing. He was a minister of the Free Will Baptist Church, having taken out his license in 1875. He was a member of the "Missouri Board", whose function is to secure a union between the Free Will Baptists and the General Baptists of Southeast Missouri.

John Wood
Birth:
Nov. 23, 1829
Virginia
Death:
Jan. 26, 1903
Doe Run, St. Francois County,
Missouri
Burial:
Doe Run Memorial Cemetery,
Doe Run,St. Francois County,
Missouri

John Wood was born Randolph County, Va. He was married in 1850 to Fidelia Nichols. Of their seven children one was commissioner of schools in California. His early education was limited. With commendable devotion he learned to read after

Merl Wright
Birth:
Jun. 3, 1903
Cassville, Barry Co. Missouri
Death:
May 6, 1977
Wichita, Kansas
Burial:
Oak Hill Cemetery, Cassville,
Barry County, Missouri

She was born June 3, 1903, near Cassville. After her ordination, she and Winford Davis established Merl's Chapel Church on Nov. 14, 1929, north of Cassville.

Rev. John Lorn Yancey (1875-1948)

Rev John Lorn Yancey
Birth:
Jun. 11, 1875
Jasper County
Illinois
Death:
Jul. 27, 1948
Fredericktown
Madison County
Missouri
Burial:
United Methodist Church
Cemetery
Fredericktown
Madison County
Missouri

1875--1948

Rev. John Lorn Yancey

Rev. John Lorn Yancey was born in Jasper County, Illinois on June 11, 1875, and passed away at his home on July 27, 1948, at the age of 73 years, one month and 16 days. On July 16, 1896 he was united in marriage to Sarah Clarinda Francis and to this union nine children were born, four girls and five boys. Four of the children preceded him in death.

He is survived by his widow, Sarah Yancey, and five children: Mrs. Grace Coomer of Caruthersville; James Monroe Yancey of this city; Rose Etta Cooper of Hot Springs, Ark.; Floyd Roland Yancey, whose present whereabouts are unknown; and Wm. Edward Yancey of this city. He is also survived by two brothers, Harry of St. Louis and Clifford of Worthington, Indiana; several grandchildren and great-grandchildren, and a host of friends. He was a devoted father and was loved by all who knew him. He was converted June 13, 1913, and was appointed a deacon by the Catharine Church the same year. He was an ardent Christian worker, and God called him to the ministry to preach the Gospel in January, 1914; He had preached in and around Fredericktown for the past 35 years.

. . . . -rmington, Mo.
1948

Yancey, Rev. John Lorn
Born: June 11, 1875
Died: July 27, 1948
Parents:
Married: Sarah Clarinda Francis
Burial: Methodist Church Cemetery (Page 91)

Rev William H York
Birth:
Jul. 25, 1897
Death:
Mar. 14, 1935
Burial:
Pleasant Grove Cemetery
Greenfield
Dade County
Missouri

A Free Will Baptist minister, who was from Hannon, MO, in 1925, when he attended the Cooperative General Association, and his name appears in in the ministers' list in its Minutes. Worked in Western Mo, and SE Kansas Associations-- Wagoner Church, and Stockton Church.

Ferrell C Zinn
Birth:
Aug. 28, 1902
Death:
Mar. 24, 1984
Burial:
Brown Cemetery, Cedar creek,
Taney County, Missouri

He was a Free Will Baptist minister and schoolteacher in southern Missouri. He was an active contributor to the *Free Will Baptist GEM* and served on various committees and boards of the state Association.

On that bright and cloudless morning when the dead in Christ shall rise,

And the glory of his resurrection share;

When his chosen ones shall gather to their home beyond the skies,

And the roll is called up yonder, I'll be there.